The SEVENTEENTH *Child*

LINNET BOOKS ✽ 1998

The
SEVENTEENTH
Child

DOROTHY MARIE RICE &
LUCILLE MABEL WALTHALL PAYNE

Library of Congress Cataloging-in-Publication Data

Rice, Dorothy Marie, 1948–
    The seventeenth child / by Dorothy Marie Rice and Lucille Mabel
Walthall Payne.
        p.   cm.
    Summary: The oral history of the seventeenth child of black sharecroppers,
describing her life in Virginia and New Jersey during the Depression.
    ISBN 0-208-02414-X (lib. bdg. : alk. paper).
    1. Payne, Lucille Mabel Walthall, 1929–
—Childhood and youth—Juvenile literature.   2. Afro-American women—
Virginia—Pittsylvania County–Biography—Juvenile literature.   3. Afro-
Americans—Virginia—Pittsylvania County—Biography—Juvenile literature.
4. Afro-Americans—Virginia—Pittsylvania County—Social life and customs—
Juvenile literature.   5. Depressions—1929—Virginia—Pittsylvania County—
Juvenile literature.   6. Country life—Virginia—Pittsylvania County—Juvenile
literature.   7. Pittsylvania County (Va.)—Biography—Juvenile literature.
8. Pittsylvania County (Va.)—Social life and customs—Juvenile literature.
[1. Payne, Lucille Mabel Walthall, 1929–   —Childhood and youth.   2. Afro-
Americans—Biography.   3. Women—Biography.]
I. Payne, Lucille Mabel Walthall, 1929–   .
II. Title.
F232.P7R53   1998   98-28614
975.5'66500496073'0092—dc21   CIP
[B]   AC

The paper used in this publication meets the minimum requirements of
American National Standard for Information Sciences—Permanence of Paper for
Printed Library Materials, ANSI Z39.48—1984. ∞

Designed by Abigail Johnston
Printed in the United States of America

To the children of Pency and George Walthall,
especially Lillie Margaret, Missouri Virginia,
Coolidge, and Clara Ann;
to the children of Mabel: Calvin, Alfred,
Patricia, Gwendolyn, and Pency;
to the numerous grandchildren,
great grandchildren, nieces, nephews,
and other kin

The fields were hard to plow;
the rows were rough to work;
the dusty roads were hard to walk;
the mountains in our lives were hard to climb;
but joy came in the morning.

—Mabel

Preface

Dorothy:

On Sunday afternoon visits to my mother's house, she and my father would tell us the most engaging stories about growing up during the Depression. The stories provoked laughter and tears. I suggested that we put them in writing. We began around 1990. From writing, we began taping the stories. From taping, we went to editing. From editing, we went to submitting them for publication.

These stories are told in a series of vignettes, or episodes, in my mother's own words. Some of the attitudes of her times will seem unfamiliar, or even wrong, to young people today, sixty years later. Perhaps her vocabulary will need some thinking about, such as words like "haints" and "ramshack." Sometimes her voice is just like poetry.

No matter what, you can be sure her stories are authentic. Like most children, she was playful and full of mischief and good humor. She was just a little girl growing up in hard times, but she was optimistic, and observed her world accurately. My mother's life, as she tells it here, was poor in possessions but full and rich with love, work, and play.

Mabel:

The purpose of this book is to share my childhood in the rural South with my children, to show them that you overcome the obstacles in your life through faith and hard work. We knew we would overcome. We knew we would not live a hard-scrabble life forever because we had hope, and faith. Our preachers encouraged us with biblical scripture. We had relatives up North who lived better and gave us hope. Our desire was to go north as soon as we were able to. This is our story.

Introduction: Hoover Times

I was born Lucille Mabel Walthall in the rural
village of Glenland in Pittsylvania County,
Virginia, on February 24, 1929. My birth was eight
months before "Black Tuesday," also known as the
Stock Market Crash, which began the Great
Depression of the 1930s.

My family were sharecroppers. That means we
were farmers who did not own our own land. We
worked for the owners of large farms. We had to
give back half of our tobacco and corn profits to
the owners, who were white. Many of them were
not wealthy either, and they were generally kind
and fair. The year I was born, income for each
person in America was $750. For farm people it
was $270; for sharecroppers, only $135. We were
poor, and about to be poorer.

At that time, Southern society was racially segregated. For us, segregation seemed natural. We
didn't know why we were separated from the
whites. It was just accepted. When I was growing

Mabel's Genealogy

George Washington Walthall
1865?-1948
(with Millie Gilbert)
Gracie 1894–1986
Robert 1896–1943
Hattie 1897?–1948
Elsie 1898?–1956

(with Pollie Lovelace)
Isabel 1909–died as infant
Susie 1910–1992

Pency Gregory
1886-1946
(with Edward Brown)
Edna 1907–1974
Jerry 1908–1935
Claude 1909–1986

George and Pency Walthall's Children
Mary 1915–1935
Lillie Margaret 1916–
Missouri Virginia 1917–
Beatrice 1921–1945
Coolidge 1925– ⎫
Calvin 1925–died as infant ⎬ twins
Katherine 1927–1975
Lucille Mabel 1929–
Clara Ann 1931–

up, everybody was poor in our area and we all worked hard, even us children. We all wore patches on our clothes. White children were shoeless, and so were we. That's all we knew. We had our own restaurants, schools, and churches. But we did feel the injustice at times, especially when we had worked together, eaten together, and some of us had even slept in the same room together — but when time came to go to school, the white children rode the bus and we had to walk.

I attended a racially segregated one-room school with primary through seventh grades. One teacher taught us all. The school was on the Glenland Baptist Church property. We had to buy our own books and supplies. We walked six miles to and from school each day. My sisters, brother, and neighbors walked together.

From what I can remember from my childhood, the word among the people was that things had been good until Herbert Hoover became the president in 1929. After the Great Depression had started, the farmers could not get a good price for their tobacco crops. There was little or no money to buy fertilizer, so sharecroppers and farmers tried making their own. The tobacco and corn crops dried up.

I remember people bartering for staple items. They went to Chatham, the county seat, for "Relief"—to get a barrel of flour and cornmeal. They were given two pigs for each family. We called them "peanut pigs" because they were very tiny and hard to grow, but there wasn't much to feed them anyway. There was very little left over from the table scraps to give them. The men were always trapping rabbits and hunting squirrels, groundhogs, and 'possums for the family meals.

To get by, people were truly creative. They would sew four fertilizer bags together to make sheets and bed ticks. The bed ticks were sacks, like large pillowcases, the size of a mattress, filled with straw. But they could not be filled too often because the cattle had to be fed most of the straw and hay. There was not enough corn and wheat to feed the animals.

For clothing, the men's long underwear were cut off when they got holes in the knees and elbows. They were used to make undershirts for the children. When the men's heavy wool socks were worn out at the heel and toe, the top part was used for children's gloves to keep their hands warm.

In 1932, Mr. Franklin Delano Roosevelt became president. He tried to solve the country's problems by using government money to help the people. They called this the "New Deal." Programs like the Works Progress Administration (WPA) and the Civilian Conservation Corps (CCC) brought work to the people who had no jobs. There was relief for farmers, too, because the government helped them to raise their crops so they could get better prices for them. But I was just a little girl and all I could see was that the hardest times were slowly beginning to ease up.

By 1936, the tobacco was growing bigger. Corn stalks produced more ears of corn, and gardens were fresh and green. More beans grew on the vines, too, and all because farmers were given fertilizer they did not have to pay for until their tobacco crops were sold. Food became plentiful. The cows gave more milk and cream, so we had plenty of butter. Pigs grew larger due to the corn feedings. We had plenty of meat, then: pork chops, neck bones, spare ribs, ham, bacon. Mr. and Mrs. Roosevelt were God-sent people for us. They helped the poor.

Even so, my family decided to move north to New Jersey to find better opportunities. That was in 1937, but things were very bad there, as far as jobs were concerned. Back in Virginia we had our own gardens. In New Jersey, we had to go to the Welfare for food. So we returned to Virginia in 1939 because my parents were farmers: that's all we knew.

This book tells what growing up in those "Hoover Times" was really like. It is a picture taken from my own life of strong and good people, and how they worked together to survive hard times.

We were told that the bottom would come to the top
just like the cream on the milk.
When the cream comes to the top,
that's where your good rich butter comes from.

—Mabel

The Seventeenth Child

I am the seventeenth child from four marriages: the knee baby. By the time I was born, in 1929, there were sisters and brothers old enough to be my parents. Some were almost as old as my mother. My mother, Pency Gregory Brown Walthall, had been married once before. She had had three children. She was forty-two when I was born. Momma was tall and shapely. My sister, Edna, her oldest daughter, used to buy her clothes. She was always stylish and neat. When I got older, I used to cornbraid her hair, put a row all around her head. She liked to wear it that way to church. She had heavy hair, gray. People called her Aunt Pency.

My father, George Washington Walthall, was known by many names. His friends called him "Six", because he was over six feet tall. He was also known as "Partner Wash" and "Uncle Wash." He had been married two times before. He must have been a frisky old man. He had long, wavy hair. All the women were after him. My father was an old man when I was born. He could have been, I guess, my grandfather. My father said he was born free. He was a 'Publican*; born the year the slaves were set free. My Uncle Leonard who was ten years old at that time had been a waterboy as a slave. He said they were brought from Campbell County. But anyway, my father, he was a strong old man, sixty-four years old, and a farmer, and we went from one place to another. We seldom stayed anywhere longer than a year.

I want you to know that my mother and father were never afraid of the white people, like a lot of people was. That's why we were always moving. That's how we got to know so many people. My father, if he didn't like something, he would speak up and he would never keep us out of school to help on the farm. We had these cousins, and they were schoolteachers. And they used to say, "Uncle Wash, are the children in school? Make sure the children stay in school."

So we would work on the farm after school.

*Republican

Just Like Old Lady Hatcher

I was born in Glenland, a little place called
Glenland, at Hatcher Farm, in a three-room house
or shack so they used to tell me, "You are just like
Old Lady Hatcher." That's where I was born, on
her plantation. That's what we called it, but it was
like a large farm today. I came down with the
pneumonia, almost died. And this little black
woman, Aunt Courtney Lewis, the midwife, who
had "lots of bread on her teeth," she delivered me.
My sisters and brothers used to poke fun at me.
She was a nice lady, but an ugly lady. My sisters
and brothers used to make fun of me because this
lady with rotten teeth had delivered me. She delivered me but never turned my name in so I didn't
get my birth certificate until 1969. It was like an
affidavit. My older sister, Missouri, had to witness
or acknowledge my birth.

I was born with curly hair, Momma said. The fever
took it out as a little girl. Because of the pneumonia
my parents were always afraid that I might catch a
cold. And later I would threaten my mother and

sisters by saying, "I'm going outside with no coat so that I can catch a cold and then you won't have me anymore." But I couldn't get away with threatening my father.

Bobbit Town

My first memory was being in another location, they called it Bobbit Town. It was in Glenland. I was told times were very hard. Everybody was poor. Poor white, poor black. It was five houses there in Bobbit Town. We lived in the storehouse and the house down the hill had the little hungry children. And at the bottom of that hill lived the white family. That was a bigger house, and over to the left was Aunt Tilde and her three granddaughters, two sons, and daughters. And then up the hill a little further was another white family who lived in a shack, a little better shack than where we had lived before. At one time there had been a store, surrounded by three small homes and two large ones.

The Neighbors

The little house with two rooms, down the hill, had
two parents, five boys and one girl: good-looking
children. Their mother was a beautiful black
woman who later died in an accident, a car accident. The father was, as they used to say, "half
white," a very poor provider. His boys always did
the hard work; the younger ones were always
begging for bread.

The third black family, they had older sons from
what I can remember. There was no husband. No
one never said anything. The mother we called
Aunt Tilde, busy as she could be in everybody's
business. She had a daughter called Big Mamma:
loose with the booty. The two white families lived
in the bigger houses. One white family was all of
seven and the white family down the hill had mules
and wagons and equipment, equipment to farm
with. One of the boys from the family of seven and
the begging black boy ate so many green apples
they died from the flux, as we called it. But it was
the diarrhea.

"Don't Break My Mirror!"

We lived in the old storehouse. Had two large rooms and a large attic, which was also used for four beds. Downstairs: one large bedroom. When I say bedroom, it was two to three beds in a room, and a pallet on the floor. Sometimes the kitchen also had a bed in it, plus a stove, kitchen cabinet, table with two chairs: one each for Momma and Daddy, two long benches on each side for we children. It was like a picnic table with benches. Daddy must have made them. And a black cook stove which a fire seemed to always have been in, and a woodbox. Momma's prized possession was one dresser and mirror.

"Don't break my mirror," she would say. She would guard that mirror with all her might no matter where we moved.

All of Daddy's older children were married with children our ages and older than us. My mother's older children were grown and living up North in Washington, D.C., or in New Jersey. In our house,

it was eleven people. Besides my parents, Aunt
Florence, Mary, Missouri, Beatrice, Katherine,
Coolidge, Clara, and myself, there was Aunt Nan
Smith, a little old lady who wore a skullcap all the
time. She slept in the corner of the kitchen of our
house. She was very polite. I don't remember too
much about her. After she passed away, my father
and the neighbors made a wooden box to put her
body in, put it on a wagon, and the neighbors
followed, walking behind the wagon, to where she
was buried, at Glenland church.

Always, Forever, Washing Dishes

My Aunt Florence lived with us. When I was born
she was already in the house. We used to call her
Totie. She had epileptic seizures and sometimes we
were afraid of her or pretended that she was after
us. She was very smart though and helped us with
our homework. She learned every song they sang
in church. She was always, forever, washing
dishes. She loved to pick up chips. Chips were

pieces of wood that was cut out of trees.
Everybody used to collect them to start fires in the
chilly mornings. There was this one particular fella,
he used to work for a white family across the road
at the other plantation. She could hear his ax
singing.

She used to say, "I'm going over, Sister Pency, to
pick up some chips to start the fire." That went on
for a while. But finally I understood, when she had
a baby for this fella. I think the baby was stillborn.
I never did see it. Eventually she got married to an
old shrivelled up guy. I couldn't understand why
everybody was so excited about her marrying this
guy. He ended up being very mean to her.

Our House

Sometimes it would be made from logs with clay in
between and maybe one or two windows. You did
not need windows really because the cracks were
in the wall and you could see people coming by
looking through the walls. All you had to do was

run to the wall and say, "Momma, here come Aunt Jane, or Uncle Tom." How do you know? Because you're looking through the cracks. You didn't need windows. Sometimes the boards were separated and upstairs there was snow and the rain. We'd put buckets and let the rain come in the buckets to keep the rain from going to the first floor and we would use that rain for doing the laundry. We used to set barrels and buckets out alongside the house to catch the rainwater. And that was less water you had to bring in. And when the rain started falling we'd run and get these buckets and tubs so we could have the rainwater.

Cinnamon and Others

We had another lady who would come by to see us, and they called her Cinnamon. She used to sleep in the barns during the warm summer months, and in the wintertime she would come to people's houses for shelter. She was one of the people that my mother put up, too, from time to time. She used to sleep in the haystacks and in the barns wherever she was. But in the meantime, there was always room for one more in our house.

My Aunt Katherine came up from Richmond one time to live with us and she brought her grandson. I remember her always wearing a bonnet. But later when I visited her in a nursing home in Richmond, she was wearing a skullcap like the nuns used to wear. She was always telling Daddy to leave Glenland and come to Richmond to live, where we could live better. Well, she had this grandson. He was the meanest little gray-eyed fella you'd ever seen in your life. He was about sixteen. He was always in trouble. He was always picking on me. Yet, she said I was the biggest crybaby she ever heard.

I Was Some Kind of a Child

I was some kind of a child. Every night I would fall asleep at the table and somebody would have to carry me out and then one night they decided to leave me in there after they finished washing the dishes. They took the kerosene lamp and left me alone in the kitchen so when I woke up I was alone. That stopped me from falling asleep at the table.

When I used to get into trouble sometimes, I would hide from my father. On one particular day I had gotten into some trouble and I knew he was going to get me. When I had found out he had gone and got the switch to whip me, I hid in the woodbox behind the stove. Then I fell asleep. They were looking for me everywhere. When they finally found me, it was that afternoon when they were getting ready to start the fire in the kitchen stove and there I was. What a mess! But I got away with it again. He was glad to see me.

Around the Hearth

So anyway, we all lived in one big, happy house in Glenland. It had a fireplace. It was beautiful. We enjoyed it to the highest. But it wasn't just for the beauty. It was useful. A lot of times, my parents did not have ten cent for kerosene for the lamps, so the fire would throw off enough light so we could sit around the hearth, or lay down sometimes and do our homework by the light of the fireplace. I never remember going to school without us doing our homework. I helped Katherine, too. I didn't want her to get a beating the next day in school for not having her homework done. I used to help my sister Katherine with her homework because she was very slow. So at night, my father used to say, "Go to bed!" It would be any hour after the sun went down.

Everybody used to go to bed at the same time. There was no such thing as you go stay up while I go to bed. So while in bed, I would try to help Katherine with her alphabet and her homework and he could hear us. He would holler upstairs, "Go to bed!" And one of my sisters would call out: "Tell him you're in bed."

Then I would repeat, "I'm in bed."

And he would say again, "I said go to bed!"

"We're in bed," I would say.

So he would come upstairs with a stick, and we would wrap up in the cover, and roll behind the bed so he couldn't get us. He'd be trying to get us underneath the bed, but he couldn't get us. Then he'd go on downstairs. But he would make up for it the next time.

Ashcakes in the Fireplace

The fireplace also played a big part as far as cooking. A lot of times my mother would rake back the ashes, put sweet potatoes into the ashes where they would cook. My father would tell my mother to make some crackling bread. She would make the cornbread, and he would take it, rake the ashes back to make a space, and then he would take the cornbread dough and throw it in and cover it with the ashes. It would bake nice and brown and crisp. She would take it out, wash off the ashes real good, and let me tell you! Talking about something good! We would get buttermilk and eat that ashcake. And boy oh boy, we had a meal!

Bully Cush

My father was forever cooking when my mother left the house. He used to make this stuff called "bully cush." I guess it was mush. It was leftover bread with water, fried meat grease, salt and pepper. He would also use leftover cornbread. We would eat that for lunch until my mother came home from work. When things got better and we started eating a little better, food was plentiful: molasses, biscuits, salmon cakes, homemade bread, fried chicken for breakfast, fatback. You name it, we had it. Sometimes if there was only one egg, my mother would take brown gravy and break the egg up in it and we would eat that. We called it "sopping the gravy." But Daddy, too, wanted us to use our forks, rather than our fingers. He wanted us to cut it up and use our knife and fork.

Every Sunday night we had to say a prayer. We would all get on our knees and say a prayer. Even if we had guests coming, they would be outside knocking. They would have to stay outside until we finished praying. And that prayer could be longer than ever, because he knew they were outside waiting.

Sister Mary

We all had the same problems. My sister Mary was retarded and also the busy neighbors had a son, the same way. My sister became more and more disturbed. She and the neighbor's son were taken to Central State Hospital, mental state hospital. It was a very, very sad day for our family and the neighbors. I inherited Mary's white iron bed. She was nineteen when she left home. Now Mary lies in an unmarked grave with just a number on it in a Petersburg cemetery. I later got her death certificate. We were all supposed to go down and have a memorial service for her, but it was never done. She really loved us children and wouldn't let anybody bother us. She wouldn't even allow my father to punish us.

Katherine, the Fox

My favorite sister was Katherine. I loved her so much. They used to call her "the fox" because she had red hair and red skin. That's what we called people who were neither dark nor too fair. She also had gray eyes like my grandfather, Jerry. All of my father's older children had gray eyes, too. But we loved each other. She and I were very close. We used to get into a lot of mischief jumping off barn lofts. It's a wonder any of us survived. One little fella started to school one day, and he said he wanted him a girl. Somebody said, "There are plenty of girls here."

But he stammered, "Me-Me-Me don't want no black gal. Me-me-me don't want no white gal. Me want a red gal."

And somebody said, "Don't forget Katherine, the fox. She is the only one. She is the reddest girl we know that you can have."

In the Hog Pen

We climbed the trees and would ride the trees to the ground and then Katherine fell in the hog pen. Almost killed her. On that poplar tree, she thought she had found a smooth tree. And by the time she got to the top, the top broke out and she fell right into the hog pen, in the trough, right where they feed the hogs at. She could have broke her back. I don't know how she survived. We didn't do things like kids do today, try to kill each other. We'd climb the trees, put a rope on it and make a swing, and things like that.

Sister Bea, Witches and Haints

Then there was Sister Bea, she was always a busy girl; she was a pretty girl. She was the oldest one left at home at that time, so we used to do a lot of following her around. She hated cats.

She taught us that there were witches and haints.*

* "haunts," or ghosts

We would pass this old lady's house, which was a cousin of my mother's. Bea told us that the old lady would take her hair off at night, and that she had no hair on her head. The next morning, she would put her hair back on her head and would stick pins in it. We learned to be afraid of her. We didn't know what a wig was, and we thought she was a witch. We were told that she was and that all old people were haints and witches. She was not a witch, we learned later on.

One night in bed we thought a witch had got on us. I was just hollering that the witch had me and Daddy said, "Hold onto it, hold onto it."

I'd say, "I got it. I got it." That's when he came in with the lamp and he discovered that I had hold of somebody's hand or foot.

Then he would say, "Shut up, gal, and go to sleep!" Then he would go on back downstairs.

Daddy's Poppa

My father used to go to work for the WPA. The WPA was the Works Progress Administration which was created by President Roosevelt to provide jobs for the farmers. Daddy worked to clear the land of bushes and trees to make roads. And I can remember so well my mother would pack my father's lunch in a half-gallon bucket. It was only fried meat or bacon you would call it now, put between biscuits.

So he would go to work and eat what he could but he couldn't eat the skin on the meat and we called it "poppa". On the way home we would meet him and we would say "Daddy, let me have your poppa today," not knowing that the poor old soul was tired and had tried to eat it but couldn't, his teeth was so bad.

So we used to ramshack his little half-gallon bucket to see what we could find in there. There wasn't always something there, but we'd eat the leavings, whatever we could anyway. It would taste good to us because there wasn't too much food at that time.

What If a Bull Would Come?

When we would be going from one house to another, on the plantation, we might see a bull loose in the pasture and we'd start asking questions: What would you do if the bull got after you? Climb the tree. Well, he can dig up a tree too, and the tree would fall. And then what would you do? We don't know what we would do. And we'd just start to running, jumping from one tree limb to another. I still have nightmares about that thing. Trying to get away from the bulls and the horses.

Hiding Under the Quilt

We used to be always so frightened when my mother and father weren't home. We were afraid of

Gypsies that used to come around. They did steal a boy one time at the circus. We never did see him again for thirty years. We were also afraid of tramps. In the fall of the year they would be coming through, traveling south. One was called Pegleg, because he had a wooden leg. We could hear his footsteps on the porch.

Daddy would say, "Don't let anybody in, because it's time for Pegleg to come through." He would come through our area every fall of the year. You could hear his wooden leg hitting the hard ground. He would wait around the stable until Daddy got home. My mother would fix food for him and Daddy would take the food and a quilt to him in the stable. After a couple of days, Daddy would say, "Move on!"

We would imagine hearing Pegleg even after he had left. We'd drape the bed with the quilt and we'd hide under the bed all day. My brother Coolidge would sneak out and get bread and come back. We would eat the bread until my mother would come home.

Babysitter Blues

I had this one sister, who didn't like to babysit. My
mother used to make her babysit and she would go
and complain. She always had some complaint, or
pretended to be sick, because she didn't like to go
out to work, so she would have to babysit. As a
little girl, I remember, she used to get so angry with
us because she had to babysit. She would say, "I'm
going to take a rope and hang myself. I'm going to
jump out of the window to kill myself." We didn't
know that the window was only two feet off the
ground and that she would never use the rope, so
we cried and begged her not to do that. We
promised to be good.

Hobo Brother

But then I had an older brother, Claude. He used
to hobo. A hobo was a person that would go from
one place to the other looking for work. They
didn't have money for train fare, so they would
catch a freight train when it was moving slow, and

hitch a ride in a boxcar. That way, they would also have a place to sleep. He would come in and out. My mother, she would pack him a lunch, but she never knew when he was coming or going. He would hop a train and travel from place to place that way.

Then one day he would just show up and she would be so happy to see him. He would eat like a pig when he got home. It seemed he could not get enough to eat. So he would stay two or three days, maybe a week or so, maybe longer. He would eat and eat and eat, and then one day he would say, "Well, Mother, I have to go," and she would get up the next morning, pack him a lunch, pack him cooked beans; you name it. She would have it in these buckets for him, because she didn't know when she would see him again. And she used to always pray for him.

She used to warn him, "One day you're going to end up with arthritis. You'll be so crippled up." And he did get arthritis. He ended up in a wheel-chair when he got old. But my brother, he was always a good boy. I loved him. He made a good living through the years. One thing about Claude I loved, was he always encouraged me. Years later, he tried to get Momma to let me stay in New Jersey and go to boarding school. "Mabel is smart. She's gonna be something," he would say.

The Devil's Keyhole

We were told that the Devil could come in through the keyhole but we were never allowed to say the word "Devil." We were allowed to say "Badman." So as the time went on, my sister Katherine and my baby sister and myself were going across the field where my parents were working, when my sister Clara looked up and said, "Children, watch out for the Devil!"

And I screamed out and I looked up in the tree and I saw this thing waving in the air and I said, "Oh, there's the Devil now!"

My sister Katherine took off running with Clara on her back. Then she got caught underneath the barbed wire fence, and the people came running from the field. They thought something really had happened. When I pointed out where I saw the Devil they started to laugh. But my mother, she really wanted to kill us.

Big Snow, 1935

Little by little things got a little bit better, and we were able to survive. One winter day my father looked out; it was kind of hazy. He says, "Its going to snow today and we need to get the wood in. You kids will have to stay home." So my brother and older sister got the axes. My father sharpened the axes. My brother and sister took the axes and chopped down trees as big across as gallon buckets. We took the limbs off and chopped them up for firewood. My sister Katherine and I dragged each tree to the woodpile. Later my sister borrowed a saw and my brother sawed up loads and loads of wood and we stacked it on the porch. Plus picking up the chips, we were busy trying to get prepared for the snow. We had a porch for a change and that was one of the nicest places we lived. Thank God, Daddy had a warning. The next morning we woke up and we had about three feet of snow.

I mean it was a deep, deep snow. Our older sisters and brothers would put us in these pans and tubs and we would slide down the hill. What fun we had! So my brother, he had forced his feet into my sister's boots. My older sister Edna, who lived in Washington, D.C., had bought the boots for Katherine. Anyway, the boots got ice in them and Coolidge could not get the boots off because the ice had packed down in the boots. He could not pull them off. He came home crying, so finally my father said, "I have to cut them off." My sister, she had a fit; but he cut them off.

Then he said, "You will have low-topped galoshes." That's what she ended up with to get the boots off my brother's feet.

Measles

The men wore wool support socks. They were
gray, heavy socks. When they were worn out, my
mother and sister would cut the tops off and
make gloves for us to wear. On one day, I went
to school. I remember, I was in the primer; they
didn't have a kindergarten. I remember we
would have to read about Jack and Jill. So I was
at school that day and my sisters and brother
were at home with the measles, and I did not
want to be in school that day, so I faked that I
was sick. At that age I was faking; so now you
know, when children try to get away with things,
I know all about it. At recess I pretended that I
was ill.

So the teacher said, "Walk down the aisle, Mabel,
and let me see if you're able to walk." So I faked
that I didn't feel good and couldn't walk. Then my
sister Bea and her good friend Tiny took turns
carrying me home on their backs, and down the
road they went on their lunch hour. And on the
way I dropped my glove.

I cried out, "I lost my glove!"

My sister said, "That's too bad, Mabel. You're going home."

They threw me in the bed with my brother and sisters who had the measles. The next day or two, here I came down with the measles. And from then on, every time I saw a glass of water that was warm and had bubbles, I swore out that I was getting the measles because bubbles always made me think of the measles rash.

Wrapping Hair

On Sunday night, our hair would get wrapped for the week. We would sit on the floor for this episode. Momma and Bea would grease our hair real good and wrap our hair with white string and loop it at the ends of the hair. We used to save the string from week to week. One would wrap Katherine's hair and one would do mine. They would part the hair into sections, but instead of braiding they would take a string or cord and go around and around the hair, wrapping it from the root to the end, which would cover most of the hair. Then they would tie a knot to keep the string from slipping out the hair. It kept our hair tidy and helped make our hair grow. Our hair would remain wrapped for the week and it would stay like that. We would go to school with the wrapped hair which looked like white twigs.

On Sunday morning our hair would be unwrapped for Sunday school, and we would leave it open or braided with a little bang. With this we thought we were all dressed up. And we would wear our best dress, which we only had one; that was a Sunday dress.

Sunday Shoes

We would have Sunday shoes, patent leather which probably cost a dollar. But I would be so excited about my little shoes that I would carry a little rag in my pocket and I would wipe my shoes

all the way to church. Sometimes the older ones would be in front of me and they kept saying, "Come on, come on, Mabel. We're going to leave you." But I wanted to keep the dust off my shoes. A lot of times I would take them off and put them in my pocket or take them off and carry them in my hands until we got almost to church. That way, they would stay nice and clean and the dust would not be on them.

One time my big sister had bought me, believe it or not, a little high-topped pair of white shoes, like baby shoes. The porches then had a lot of openings—underneath cracks you would say—so as I was walking across the porch floor, my brother and his friend Crebo were under the porch. He took his knife and he sliced my little pair of shoes that I hadn't had too long and it was really upsetting. But people just didn't know how upsetting things could be for children sometimes. So even though my mother screamed at him and let him know it wasn't the nicest thing to do, no one replaced the shoes I had wanted so badly.

Sunday School

Women, the elder women, would try to teach us
the Bible. A lot of them could read and write and
some of them would memorize what was going on.
There were some there that didn't even have good
stockings, they were full of runs, but they were
doing the best they could. My mother never taught
Sunday school, but she would make sure we got
there. After Sunday school there were a lot of times
we had church. The women would get real happy,
shout, throw their babies all over the church. This
one particular lady, she would shout every Sunday.
I guess they were very depressed women who
didn't know what was going to happen from day to
day. Things were very hard for families back then.

Billy Goat Sunday

On Sundays, after church, it was the custom for
people to visit each other. The older people would
sit and talk and the children would play. A lot of
them thought they were courting. And this boy

Crebo, he had a billy goat. We were all playing, teasing this billy goat, and all at once he decided to let this billy goat go and, you're talking about a trip! Billy goats are funky, stinky! Here come the billy goat running through the house with all the children running and he ended up right along with the children upstairs. My cousin, she was trying to get the billy goat out of the room and down the steps. It was a hard problem to get the billy goat out of the house.

Sunday night was time to collect everything, such as to get your water from the spring if you had to be in before sundown. If you didn't get it in before sundown, you would have to go into the dark to bring the water in. The buckets were supposed to be filled.

Make Her Walk

Crebo also had a sister and brother. And oh, they would use such profane language. They would cuss out their mouths one minute, and they would sing

Christian songs the next. They also had another sister. This one girl, she wouldn't walk and she was seven years old. And we would ask, "Why you don't walk?"

And she would say, "I don't want to walk because if I walk, I would have to pick up chips, and I'm not going to pick up no darn chips."

So my mother told her father, "Get you a good switch, she'll get up from there and walk then."

So that's just what they tried, and she got up. She was an angry girl but she had to get up and do her share of work.

Later on, in that same house lived another family, and they had a son they called Charlie Ray, and Charlie Ray, I guess you would say, he was peculiar. And if you came from the store and he didn't know if you had candy or not, he would start climbing the trees and crying and slobbing like a mad dog until you gave him candy. And my sister Bea used to tease him all the time, but when he finally grew up, he wasn't so bad after all.

School Antics

We had to walk many miles to school. I think we really went to Christian schools because the schools were always right on the church grounds, and we used the church for our auditorium. And the church members were always coming back to help us out. Especially for our plays. They were always Christian plays. We were never without joy and happiness. I believe we were more happy, then, than ever. Our churches served as restaurants, auditoriums, whatever. They served dinners, we had conventions. Boy, did we enjoy ourselves.

At school, the older boys and girls would have to help with breakfast and the teacher would inspect each and every one of our fingernails to make sure our fingernails were clean. The older ones would inspect the younger ones and we would go through that episode and in the morning our brothers and sisters that were older were just as busy washing their hands with the soap that was given through the Health Department. I think it was Lifebuoy

soap. And they would be cleaning the dough from under their nails because they had to make biscuits in the morning and had no time to clean before they left home.

And for lunch everybody would try to share what they had, but we would have to say grace. Everyone had to say grace. And we would have to greet each other in the morning. It wasn't just "Hi," "Bye," "What you doing?" Everybody spoke English, not just the slang. If they spoke slang, it was because they didn't know any better. And then we would say our grace at lunchtime and then we'd say our goodbyes in the afternoon.

Everybody helped. The older ones helped the younger ones even though some of the younger ones were further ahead with their education. A lot of the older ones had had to stay home to help with the children.

When we were going to school, I remember the teenagers, they got beat just as much as the small children. The girls, they'd be hanging around the bushes with the teenage boys. If they didn't come back from recess at a certain time, the teacher, she would make them go back down to the bushes, get switches, and she would give them good beatings. And the parents never said one word about it.

Playtime

We used to play hide and go seek, kick the ball, kick the can, and baseball, most of the time it was baseball, and jack rocks. We used small stones instead of the metal jacks. We also used a stone instead of a ball. Jump rope, don't forget jump rope. Everyone used to jump the rope.

We had hills that we would slide down. We had to go to the spring to get water. Then we would pour water on the hill so that we could have like a sliding board.

We thought our dresses were getting dirty and muddy and we couldn't get away with that. So we would put our dresses down in our panties, and slide down the hill. We would go home so many times with our underpants so dirty. We used to show off, we little children used to show off how fast we could go down the hill in front of the older children.

If you wanted a wagon, you went into the woods and cut you a tree down, cut your wheels out of the tree, and put a hole through, put an iron through there, strap it down and make you a body to put on it. Take that thing and you'd have one of the best racing wagons, you know those things that go down the hill, and you'd be rolling. And if you wanted something you got it yourself. We used to have Tom-walkers: Take two sticks with a sprout on the side, and walk them and you have stilts. I could put a hurting on some Tom-walkers.

School Days

We all used to play together, work together, the teenagers, the black and white, but when time came to go to school we went on our separate ways. The black walked and the white rode the school buses, and so the teenagers got tired of the whites passing by and calling them names.

So one fella said, "We're going to fix them today." He told my sister, so they got some rotten eggs from the hen's nest and he hid them in the grass. That afternoon, when the bus came by and they started to call us names, we started throwing those rotten eggs and boy, what a mess! You could smell them for a mile.

Church Conventions

Sunday school conventions meant a lot because we sent delegates to the Baptist Association. Even though the neighbor churches were five or ten miles, maybe twenty miles apart, each church represented themselves from the Sunday school. Everybody was interested in participating. The young people had Baptist Youth Fellowship on Sunday night. That kept us very busy. When the convention started, people would come from far

and near, especially those that were living away from home. They would come back for the special occasion. The parents, especially the mothers, would prepare big dinners.

One neighbor, she could make such good egg custard pies, coconut pies, cakes, sweet potato pies. Momma made everything good. Her specialty was those fried sweet potato pies, the individual pies. Everybody had a specialty: fried chicken, ham. You name it, we had it on those church grounds. Everybody enjoyed themselves and it was mostly like a carnival. Because we had musicians, and we had magicians, and everybody did what they could do in performing. We had a few fights too, but we didn't worry too much about that, because the elders had that under control.

Don't Forget the Lemonade

Oh, they made tubs and tubs of lemonade at those conventions and it would be five cent a cup. Sometimes they would give it to you for free. It was so good! Ice cold. Homemade ice cream. All of those good things. I never will forget the associations. All the older people would come back home from West Virginia, Ohio, New Jersey, you name it. They would all come back. My brother Robert, he would come back. My father would be so excited when he saw that car coming in, he would say, "Oh, I know my son Robert is on his way!" Gracie, my oldest sister, the whole crew would come back. And what a reunion we used to have! Everybody just had so much fun. I'll just never forget those good days when the churches got together.

Then one day, we moved from that place to another little place called Straight Stone, where we weren't as happy with the location. We never would forget Glenland.

Tobacco Farming

We used to raise tobacco and we worked in the fields. My father and some of the other men used to

find a wooded area and they would clear the woods by cutting the trees down and digging up the tree stumps to cultivate that part. It could be a square maybe 25 x 25 feet or bigger. They would lay logs alongside that area. Then they would put the tobacco seeds in around February or March so that the rain wouldn't wash them away. Then they would cover the seeds with a cheesecloth to make sure the birds wouldn't get them or that they wouldn't get covered up by the leaves and things in that area.

So they would plant the tobacco around February and my mother would put in her turnip greens, or kale, or whatever then. We used to call it "salad" and she used to plant that on the edge of the tobacco area around May, April or May. The little tobacco plants would be dug up, ready to be put back into the ground. If it rained we would use a peg because the men would already have made the rows with the mules and plows. The men would turn the soil and make the rows real high.

Then we would take the peg: the peg was like a stick. Everyone had their own peg that they used from time to time. And if you were young, you would drop the plants, about three feet apart. Then someone, an older person, would come along, make a hole with the peg. And you'd bend over, had to bend over real low to stick the plant in the ground just right.

As you got older, you would be able to drop your plants, then go back and peg the holes yourself. Well, about maybe six weeks later, you'd go back and you'd use the hoe and knock the weeds that would grow around the grass, and weed it to keep the grass from overtaking the tobacco plant.

Suckers and Worms

Then about the time the tobacco plant got to about two feet, you would have to pull the suckers. The suckers were little growths that come in between the leaves. You'd have to take your finger and you'd break those off, so the suckers wouldn't outgrow the tobacco and the leaves would be nice and big.

And there would be another change, the worms. Some of the worms would be as big as your finger — well, say three inches — and they would sit up on the end of their tails and they would click at you because they had horns, they were angry. Well, everybody would pick the worms off the leaves. They would get a bucket or whatever, put some ashes in it, and you'd go down the rows to check each leaf and see if the worms were on the tobacco leaves because they would eat up a plant in no time. So we used to have to take those off with our hands, drop them into the bucket. Then my father would kill them or we would kill them at the end of the row.

After picking the worms off the tobacco, then came the time when you would go back to pick suckers and a lot of times, my father would put tomato plants along the tobacco rows and that would be nice because we would be able to get a tomato. But the gum would be so heavy on the tobacco when picking the suckers that your hands were always dirty, sticky, gooey. We worked in overalls, straw hats, and worn out twist-over shoes, whatever.

Cooling It

We would also go to the spring at twelve o'clock. We couldn't work any later than about eleven-thirty because we went into the fields around five-thirty or six o'clock in the morning while it was cool. Then we would come home and stay there until about two o'clock in the afternoon, if it was very hot. We had no air conditioning, but there was always a tree, or we'd throw a quilt down on the ground, and then after dinner we just laid around in the shade until it got cool. And everybody knew, you didn't have to have a watch to come in from the fields. You'd see your shadow. If you could step on your head, you knew it was twelve noon. And the mules would know when to come in. They would start going that way towards home. But most of the time we went by our shadow.

Irish Potato Pudding

We also could hear the dinner bells ringing. A lot of people had these big old dinner bells and they would hit those bells and they would ring and you could hear them from one plantation to the other, because it was a sign it was twelve o'clock, time to come in for lunch or dinner too, because you had three square meals then. And my mother would always have a beautiful meal for us. As the years went on, we never missed a dessert. She made one dessert, she had nothing else to make dessert out of, she decided to get some white potatoes—we called them "I'sh potatoes" at that time—and she used them to made the nicest potato pudding you ever tasted. It was delicious.

Pulling Tobacco

When the leaves started to look yellow or discolored, it was time for them to be taken off the stalk of tobacco. The men would make slides about three feet wide by ten feet long so it could be easy for the mule to go dragging them in between the rows. These slides had burlap sides made of fertilizer bags. They were movable so when the men put the tobacco leaves in they would not fall off or out of the slides.

Men would bring the slides with the tobacco into the shade of the trees where we would be waiting. My sister Bea did most of the tying of the tobacco on the stick. We young ones would pass around the leaves in a bundle to her. She looped the thread around the plants. She could tie up to 250-500 sticks a day with some help. A barn would hold that amount.

Rolling My Eyes

I'll never forget one day. It was early in the morning, and we were passing tobacco. You pass a stick of tobacco from one person to the other. And the green tobacco was pretty heavy because you passed it three in a bundle; and I imagine there was about eighteen bundles on a stick. And I was about six years old, no more, maybe seven, and the sun wasn't even up. I was so tired from passing these sticks, so they could be put in the barn. And I had worked the night before.

My father looked around and I was rolling my eyes because I was so tired and angry. And he said to me, "Who are you rolling your eyes at?"

"I'm not rolling my eyes, the sun is in my eyes." I lied, because the sun was barely up.

So he said, "You better not be rolling your eyes at me." That was a sign of disrespect to an adult. But he didn't realize how tired I was.

Tobacco Barns

I want to talk about the barns that they cured tobacco in. They were made of logs. The men would cut the logs and after they crossed them and put them together and left a space for a door, then they would take mud, clay, and pack it in between the logs and that's how the barns were made.

Usually at the end of the day, the men would come out of the field and help. They would put the green tobacco on the sticks in the barns. These barns had dirt floors with flues on them. These were metal pipes with holes, and they ran through the barn and

two fire boxes were on the outside. The heat from the fires came through those flues and dried out the tobacco. That's why we called it flue tobacco.

In the barns was rows of logs just two-three feet off the ground and every two feet after that, building up to maybe twelve feet high. They were long as the barn, round as half-gallon buckets, and strong enough for two men to stand on, passing the sticks of tobacco up. They were like shelves for about 500 sticks. Those sticks would lie across the logs and the leaves hang down, and cure in that hot dry place.

Bunion Stew

The next day after the barn was filled with tobacco, my father would go back to the barn and he would make a fire in the fire box, then he would let it burn slow for about two or three days. Then he'd stay at the barn all night long to watch the fire so the barn wouldn't catch on fire, and to feed the fire box so that the tobacco would dry faster. That's when we would come and join him at night in the barn, sleep under the shed and stay put with him. My mother would stay all night, and later we would have bunion stew.

A lot of people had bunion stew then. If the men had to stay overnight at the barn and cure tobacco, everybody would get together and make this stew. I also want to talk about the pot. The pot was a big wash pot, big, black wash pot that you washed, boiled your clothes in, but it was cleaned out so you could make your stew in it. And big logs of wood were put around it. That's why it took all day to cook.

It was Brunswick stew, but we used to call it bunion stew. I don't know why. If you had rabbit, you brought rabbit, squirrel, if you had chicken, if you had a piece of ham, fatback, butter beans, any kind of vegetable you had. All of that went into that pot. It would cook all day long up until about eight o'clock at night. Then everybody would pitch in. They had their little dishes and they would eat this bunion stew. And that way the men would have somebody to stay at the barns with them and in the meantime, we had a little party.

Trash Tobacco for School

After the tobacco was cured, it was taken out of the barn and it was stacked, put away until the fall. Then the men would go back to the barn where they had a pit. The barn would be kept real damp to make handling the dry tobacco easier. The dampness kept the tobacco leaves from crumbling. And you would bundle the tobacco up, tie it, and pack it down before you would take it to the market. But my mother used to wrap bundles of tobacco all day long, bless her heart. She would tie the better tobacco and Daddy would give us the trash tobacco and then he said we could have the money from the trash tobacco to buy our school supplies.

Used Books and Poor Whites

We would take the trash tobacco and the little money that came from that, that would buy our school books. And the books, we never had new books until the last year, because we always bought the used books from the white children. They were always passed down to us. Nobody ever complained about this, we were just glad to have the books. And I'm sure, we had just as much education as they had. Sometimes they couldn't go to school. But the last year in school, I remember, we were able to buy brand new books.

Some white children, poor white trash, were so filthy and lice-infested they couldn't go to school with the other whites. So my father and some other men called a meeting to allow the children to go to school with us. And Momma washed them with kerosene for the lice, cleaned them up, and they came to our school.

Sweeping the Yard

We used to sweep our yard so clean that it would be like a patio. We used dogwood brush for a broom. We swept the yards so that no grass would grow for the snakes to hide in. The snakes would slide in the house if you didn't watch and check them. Sometimes they might even get in your beds. When my sister Katherine and I were around eight and ten years old, we would go over to the Moorefields' house to sweep their yard too.

The Moorefields were wealthy and their farm seemed to be larger than the others that we worked for. Mrs. Moorefield and her family loved my mother very much. My mother had worked for them part time and she had helped deliver Mrs. Moorefield's son, Frank.

At that time fertilizer and hog feed bags were printed in color and you could buy a bag for ten cent apiece. Two bags would make a dress. Her daughter, Miss Minnie Moorefield, would make dresses for us in exchange for sweeping her mother's yard. That way we had extra dresses to wear to school.

The Moorefields also had a store where we would go to buy candy and Mr. Moorefield would let us buy the leftover candies in the jar for only two or three cents. It might be as much as a pound of hard candy for only two or three cents. We thought he was great!

Momma's Chickens

My mother used to love to raise chickens and sometimes her hen would be missing for a few weeks in the early spring. Then up come the hen with about twelve baby chicks following her from down in the woods where she had laid her eggs and hatched the chickens. My mother would be so glad to see the hen come up with the little baby chicks. She would be so excited. And that would be one of her conversations when she saw her neighbors. And then the neighbors would be eyeing the chicks until they became half-grown cause then that's when everybody in the neighborhood would get a chicken. Momma would let them have a chicken until the next family's chicken hatches, and as they hatched everybody would pay each other with a chicken.

We used to go to the store to take the chickens and trade them for beans or sugar or salt and pepper and stuff like that: just small things. We never had to have a lot of things from the store, because my father raised everything. We always had a beautiful garden. On the way to the store we would try to feed the chickens a little extra to try to make them weigh more. We'd give them a few gravels, to make their craw real heavy. My mother used to say, "Bring back five pounds of sugar" and when we'd get to the store we would buy four pounds of sugar because everything was measured out, so we could have five cent more for candy. My brother wanted golden grain tobacco because he liked to smoke. He'd say, "If you get the tobacco instead of the candy this time I'll give y'all a cigarette."

Then we'd get one cigarette. He'd say something happened to the rest and he'd hide the pack under the woodpile. He would have us looking everywhere.

He'd say, "Somebody must have gotten them while I was asleep last night."

And that was the end of the cigarettes. I'm not sorry because I never use tobacco in any form. So that doesn't bother me at all.

Stump Babies

My mother loved flowers, and when my father used to plow the garden she would say, "Make sure you leave enough room for my flowers," and that would be like a quarter of an acre. Zinnias, marigolds, whatever she could find. She became a member of the garden club later on. One year I remember my sister and I, we were wondering where babies came from. We thought they came from a tree stump and we would go from one hole to another looking for a baby under the stump. But we later found out that babies did not come from a stump because there was never anything there except for water, which the boys who used to have ringworm on their face would have to take from the stump to wash their face to get rid of the ringworm. I guess it helped because the boys were not always the cleanest things.

One day when my sister Bea had been stringing tobacco, she went into labor. My mother had to send her back home. The beautiful baby, Mae West, was born that night. My father did not want to discuss this with anyone. I remember him going out to get the midwife to come. When we woke up that night we heard this baby crying. She was the prettiest little thing you ever seen in your life. And those days you stayed in bed, after having a baby, for seven days and you stayed inside the house for a month. We were excited. She was left with us most of the time, so it was like having a little sister.

Whitewash and Polecats

We moved from Bobbit Town which was in Glenland to Clay's plantation across from where we were living and this place wasn't as nice. That was about 1935 or 36. Just three small rooms. Just before we moved in my mother went over and whitewashed the house on the inside. The whitewash was diluted white clay and water. We used

the rags and we would dip them in the whitewash
and we could all play a part in this. So we went all
over the walls and made it white and that way it
was nice and clean. My mother burned sulfur and
rags to run out the bedbugs and varmints, snakes,
rats, polecats, possum. That way the odor would
run them away.

Our neighbors were poor, poor white people, but
they had the teams which were the animals and the
plows to turn the earth to plant the crop. But my
father he never had none of this, so we just had to
be sharecroppers going from place to place.
Everybody had a lot of children in those days so
they could help on the farms.

An Old Ham Bone

My poor mother had to wash for this poor white
family. They had about four big over-strapping
boys and she would go and wash their filthy
clothes for fifty cents and an old ham bone. When I
say an old ham bone, sometimes it wasn't fit for a

dog to eat; but she would take it home, wash it real good, and boil it and sometimes cook it with a pot of beans. And there were times she would take it and throw it away. She put it in the creek of running water and no one would know she had thrown it away.

She says, "Well, you accept what they give you; next time it might be better."

It would be so cold in the shed where she'd be washing these old clothes for these people and it would be all dirty. I mean dirty, dirty. And at that time women didn't have sanitary napkins for their monthly period. You used rags torn up. She would have to wash that, too.

Sometimes I would see her spit in the water and I would say, "Momma, why do you spit in the water?"

And she would say, "That helps to get them clean."

But I know she was just so angry because she had to survive. When you have so many children you have to survive the best way you can.

With my father being a sharecropper there was very little money and sometimes there wasn't any. But at least we survived, we had the gardens and my mother would can all day in the summertime. It was never too hot to pick the beans, wash the greens, put them into the jars. If your hands were small, meaning the children, you washed the jars in tubs of water to get them prepared for canning, so we'd have food for the wintertime. Everybody could take a part in this.

Winter Work

In the cold, cold wintertime when we could not go to school we would sit around, and sew bed quilt pieces putting the tiniest, tiniest pieces together while Momma did the biggest squares. Sometimes my father would save the bags of blackeye peas so we could shell those on the days we could not go to school because the roads were so bad. They were dirt roads, no snowplows; the men would take the horses and drag the snow with a sled. Each family would do that, that wasn't too darn lazy.

And he would bring the blackeye peas bags from the smokehouse and we would have to shell peas all day or shell corn, dry corn off the cob. You could get callouses from that. Corn would cut your hands. My father wouldn't let us use the sheller because he wanted to keep us busy all day. We never had one dull moment that we didn't have to do something.

It makes me sad to think my father and my mother worked so hard and with all the hard work they did I look at myself today and I make more in one week than they made in one year of hard work, labor.

Hair

My sister Bea was always in hair, she just loved to stay in hair, and every time somebody would do a new style she would always join in. My father was

forever throwing away the straightening combs, hiding them; and then she would get a rag, ball the rag up, rub it across the stove and let it get real hot on the stove and press her hair just the same. Sometimes she would use pig feet oil, whatever she could get her hands on.

One day she came back with the boyish bob that was in style and she thought she was the cat's meow.

My sister Katherine said, "Oh, Bea looks so good, Mabel." She says, "Take the scissors, and do my hair like that." So I started to cutting, and the more I cut, it wasn't enough. Finally I looked and she just had hair above her ears and a little bit on top like a Bantam rooster. Then she became angry.

When my mother came home from work, she said, "I don't want any more playing in hair. If you do, when I come home I'm going to cut you bald."

The following day, she went to the neighbor's to help somebody out. What happened? My sister Katherine took this old, hard chewing gum that had been stuck on the bedpost for months. I don't know who it belonged to; it could have belonged to anybody because we were forever claiming somebody else's chewing gum because there was so little money to buy it. She takes the gum and sticks it in my hair. And at that time I had long hair.

And she says, "Let me cut that out because if Momma see it, she's going to give us a good beating and she is going to cut our hair bald."

Not knowing what she was doing, she cut a piece out and when Momma came home, being so tired, she saw this and she said, "Tomorrow morning I'm going to cut you girls bald."

And my sister Bea said, "Oh no, you won't. I'm going to write my brothers and sisters and tell them not to send you any more money if you cut their hair." Because they used to send money to help out.

Momma said, "Yes, I will."

Daddy said, "Don't do that."

So when he goes for a walk to visit a neighbor, what happens? She calls us in. Katherine first. She didn't have much hair left.

I jumps in the bed and I was going to be a baby and I threatened, "I am going to walk in snow again and get pneumonia so you won't have me anymore."

And then she calls me in and balds my head. And there were the locks falling off my head. I hated my mother for this. And that year for Christmas, my sister and I got overalls and we still had to go to school looking like little boys. And boy, oh boy, the kids would laugh at us, but they finally got used to it, because our hair growed back fast. From that day on, I never wanted anybody to play with my hair. I tried to take care of it myself.

Daddy

Daddy didn't show much affection. We never sat on his lap or anything like that. The only time I can remember was when we had our hair cut like boys and had gotten overalls for Christmas. We went to meet him and he was drunk. He said, "Hello, George," and he pat me on the head. George was our neighbor, and Daddy was being funny.

I guess he had feelings for us because he made sure we ate. If we were playing ball on Sunday afternoon, he would come out and backstrap, which meant umpire, and be catching the ball, you know? Even though he was an old man, he would jump out there and try to play. But he would beat the hell out you when you did something bad.

Fishing

One day my mother decided to go fishing. She was always forever wanting to find a nice fishing hole because that's what all the older women did was fish. It was like a family outing. The children would stay together trying to keep the snakes from the nursing mothers who were fishing, because the snakes, we called them cow-suckers, would smell the milk and come up to attack the mothers. I never seen it happen though. The older people would enjoy themselves fishing.

And what happened was, she found this little special fishing hole and went back with us to the fishing hole. There was a log running across this creek. She saw the fishing hole on the other side of the creek and told my brother to try the log out to see if it would hold her.

"Go across, Coolidge, see if the log is rotten and will it hold me when I cross over."

Well, she had to be a woman almost 200 pounds, so my brother being 100 pounds, maybe 125, he gets on the log and he goes across and everything is fine.

And so she says, "Okay, it will hold me." So she gets up, steps on the log, kind of prancing on it to check if it's strong enough. She gets half way and into the water she went. Then my brother jumps in and he helps her out. She was on one side of the creek and we were on the other side. We were

screaming and yelling like little calves. Up and
down the creek hollering for her because we
thought something terrible had happened to her.

Tom Buck

Well, one day Clara and my other sister, we were
out there playing and the people were in the fields
working and my mother wasn't home. Up come
this smart-aleck white boy on a horse and he said
to my sister Clara, "Move out the way." Because
she didn't move fast enough, she was only four
years old, he says, "Black so-and-so, why don't you
get out of the way?"

So we hurried her out the way. And just before he
came back we told my mother, because she had
delivered him at his birthing.

And my mother said, "What happened?" And so
we told her, and when he came through the yard,
his name was Tom Buck, she reached up on the
horse, snatched him off the horse, slammed him

down and slapped his tail real good and went over and told his mother.

His mother said, "You did just the right thing; if he come through there again talking smart to you, Aunt Pency, you do the same thing for him." And he was a boy sixteen years old.

Paper Dolls and Frog Legs

One white lady, Mrs. Robious—Tom Buck's mother—she used to save the comic strips from the Sunday newspaper for me and I would cut out Tillie the Toiler* for my paper dolls. They were always given to my mother on Monday if she went over to work for this lady. Sometimes we would get our paper dolls out of the Sears and Roebuck catalogs. We also had a dollhouse and would put the paper dolls in with the real dolls which were made of papier mâché. When the dew hit them, the other dolls appeared to break out in a rash like they had the measles.

* a popular comic strip character

I remember when my cousin and my older brother came down from New Jersey with my sisters, they were riding in an old rumble seat in a car. And I wanted to make a little extra money, so someone had taught me how to hop like a frog. Put your arms behind your knees, squat, and walk on your front legs.

I would do that and people thought I was funny, funny for a few pennies, and I would share them with my sister Katherine.

Marbles

My brother, he used to love to play marbles and he was a good marble player. So what he did, he won this boy's marbles and that afternoon just before dark, here come this boy riding on a mule with his daddy, both of them riding the mule. My mother asked what's the matter.

Then my father came out, and asks, "What's going on?"

And this boy sobs, "Coolidge took my marbles (sob)."

"Took your marbles?" my mother said.

"Yeah (sob), he took my marbles." That boy was one of my brother's favorite friends and Coolidge was forever looking out for him.

My brother says, "I didn't take his marbles, I won the marbles."

Then my mother said, "Okay, we're going to give him back the marbles."

So my father who thought so much of my brother, thought there wasn't nothing like my brother, told my brother, "Don't ever play marbles with him again."

And he didn't play with the boy anymore, even though they were friends.

Farewell

Life was beginning to get real good, tobacco was bringing a good price, the crops was good. I never seen so many beans; my mother was able to take vegetables into town to sell.

Then my sisters Lillie and Missouri, brother Claude and his wife Lena, came down from Jersey in 1937. I find this was my first time seeing Lillie, since she was twelve years older than me, and I was just two when she left home. She was just as pretty as the family had said she was. She was always writing letters, but she never came home after she left. This was her first time returning.

She wanted us to move North because she thought we could have a better life up there. But my brother Claude says no, because there was no work; the family would be better off staying in Virginia. It was worse in New Jersey than it was in Virginia at that time. Father says no. My older sister Bea says yes. So the final word was yes. On that day we had to give up everything—furniture, clothing, our friends, food—because we could not take everything.

Here come this big car with the driver and my sister, and don't let me tell the rest. Ten of us getting ready to go to New Jersey in one car. My mother had fried up chicken, it seemed, all night long. She packed lunch, cake, you name it. She had everything for us. I think the car may have been a '36, or '35 Plymouth, or maybe a Buick, and it was full. We were packed in the back of the car. Some sitting on the floor.

We carried clothing, everything Momma could possibly fit in. We left a lot of good stuff behind. She sent some by train, but we didn't have as much as we would have had if we had stayed at home. Things were really getting good then. I hated to leave home and I'm sure my brothers and sisters didn't want to leave either.

Poisoned by the Paint

Now we're on our way to Montclair, New Jersey and the driver wasn't going fast enough for my father, I guess. He was pretty cramped, being old. He kept telling the guy to go faster, go faster. The fellow was speeding. We got a ticket. We had to go back almost fifty miles to pay for the ticket.

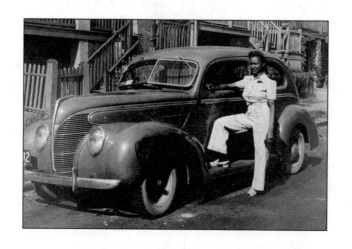

When we got to Montclair we had the most beautiful house I'd ever seen in my life: a little yellow house with a fence around and a brook running behind it. It was freshly painted. We never had seen paint before in our lives, except maybe some paint in school, finger paint. And the house was so clean. But overnight, we became ill: poisoned by the paint fumes. Everybody was very sick, but we loved the house.

We loved New Jersey very much, but there were times things were very hard and we didn't know which way the ends were going to meet. I'm sure my parents worried about it. One time we all moved in with my brother.

We moved to Paterson, New Jersey and the man would not allow us to take the furniture off the truck. This is when we moved in with my brother, Claude. We were crowded in three rooms, with him, his wife and three children. And here come another nine. That is how we were living, but we survived it. This is what life was all about: surviving. My sister-in-law, Lena, was a fine person. She never complained. She made hot chocolate and oatmeal every morning; sent us to school. She was very good to us. I loved her very much.

Now That You're Here, You Should Stay

When we finally moved again to Forest Avenue in Paterson, we had a place of our own. We had a five-room apartment. We met a lot of nice people in the neighborhood and school. Things, we thought, were getting a little better. But my father had had enough. He would walk from Montclair to Newark and from Newark to Montclair about ten miles each day and he couldn't get a job. Nobody could get a job. There just wasn't any work in New Jersey at this time: the Irish and Italians were fighting for jobs. Already my father was close to seventy years old, but he was still seeking work.

He says, "I have to go back to Virginia, I can't survive here. I need to go back."

And my mother said, "We'll try a little while longer."

And my brother Claude said, "Why don't you just stay? Let Coolidge keep working for Dr. Green. And Clara can stay with you, Mother. And let Mabel go off to boarding school, she's smart. Now that you're here, you should stay."

Dr. Green was a dentist we used to help. The biggest thing we did was empty trash and play Chinese checkers. I was a whiz at Chinese checkers.

My sister, Lillie, thought that bringing us there would help us, but it was a bad time to make a move. She and her husband were not working. My sister Suh, that's what we called Missouri, was trying to do all she could to help us, but she had a full-time job, with only Wednesdays off.

My sister Bea had her baby Mae so she could not work. When she was on the farm, she had had certain things to do. My other sisters and brothers would get so angry because she would not work, not even in a pie shop, and the child had to be fed. She was not used to city life, so she tried to gather all the city things she could at that time. My mother would think that she had gone looking for a job and she would be in New York City having a good time with her friends. She was a very outgoing, friendly girl.

And Ten Cent Was a Lot of Money in Those Days

I loved New Jersey and I sure hated to leave it because I had made a lot of friends. I had Maryanne who was a nice little white girl who taught me how to roller skate. Every Wednesday I would meet the trolley car on the corner and hit my older sister, Suh, for ten cent—a lot of money in those days—and I would go out and buy ice cream cones for Maryanne and me. We would just go roller skate all the afternoon. I would help my retarded neighbor, Dorothy, across the railroad tracks to school and her father would give me a dollar a week. That dollar was used for the house; and my mother might give me, maybe, ten cent, because bread then was ten cent a loaf. So that made it real nice.

We also used to have to take turns going to Bingo. The younger sisters going with the older sisters. I won five dollars and couldn't claim it because I was too young; but finally we brought it home. Five dollars was big bucks, but I owed everybody. By the time I finished paying off and giving it to Momma, I had maybe fifty cent left.

We Had to Return to Virginia

But around March 1939, Daddy caught the train to Virginia, lived in a barn, worked for fifteen dollars a month and when school was out, we had to return to Virginia. It was time to say goodbye to New Jersey. We caught the train. I never had been on a train, or inside a train station before. The big Penn Station in New York there had escalators, and boy, we were afraid to get on those!

We caught the train back to Virginia and moved in with my sister Elsie. We stayed there about two months. She had a big family: there were twenty of us in four rooms. We had pallets, beds. Wherever you could put them, they were there. We slept on coats. And there were so many chinches, bed bugs so big and fat we named them after cars — Fords, Cadillacs. They would suck everybody's blood, bite you, and run.

Making Do

We lived there until we moved into our own place that my father had rented for three dollars a month. It was without the furniture we had left when we went to New Jersey. We were never able to collect that. So my father made a bed for my mother out of two-by-fours, a bunk. We moved into this little house. And the rest of us slept on the floor on pallets.

My father used to buy chairs sometimes and they were wicker-weaved. They would wear out as time went on. He would have this old man that would come by to reweave the bottoms of the chairs. The old man, he would take chicken, ham, meat or whatever. Sometimes my mother would give him eggs to bottom the chair because we never had the money to pay him unless it was in the fall of the year after selling tobacco.

Then we would help in the field; help people in the tobacco for fifty cent a day. Some man would be paying sixty cents and we would go over there for a day. We would have to go there early in the morning. First we would have to get water and make sure my mother was okay for the day. Momma was productive. She saved everything she could get her hands on. Sometimes she would go with us, and we would work all day long and come home late at night.

Young and Restless

In 1943 I returned to New Jersey to babysit for my sister, Suh.

"Why should you babysit, when you can get a job and you can help Aunt Pency?" my cousin Hewitt

asked. "You are only fourteen, but I can get an affidavit stating you are sixteen to get a job."

So that's just what he did and I went to work at Maidenform Brassiere Company making twenty-seven dollars a week. That was big bucks, let me tell you! I sent money home to my mother. I met a lot of friends, and a nice fella that I thought I was in love with. I had a suit in lay-away for the first time. Then we got a telegram that my brother Robert, my father's oldest son, had gotten killed in the mines in Welsh, West Virginia, or it could have been Bluefield. And we had to return to Virginia for the funeral. I hated to leave New Jersey. I had a feeling I would not return.

Sure enough, I did not return. My mother said, "If you can make that kind of money, Katherine is older, so she should be able to make more. Now that you're home, you need to go back to school."

A Diploma for a Sugar Stamp

Okay. I felt terrible. I felt like my world had caved
in. I never did forgive my mother for that. I felt
that she was taking my opportunity away from me.
There was a white schoolteacher who lived on the
next farm from us. She needed a babysitter.

"She wants you to babysit for her and she'll teach
you in the afternoon. You will get your diploma for
the seventh grade. And you will be able to gradu-
ate," my mother told me.

That's just what I did. That went on for a whole
nine months. I worked for this lady babysitting.
She would teach me and give me two dollars and a
half per week for babysitting. In the afternoon she
would give me homework. In the morning before
leaving I would have to help my mother with the
chores and with my sister Clara, who was twelve,
and my niece, Mae, who was about seven years old
then. They had to go to school. I would put them
on my brother's bicycle: ride Clara on the back of
the bike, and Mae on the handlebars. I would give

them a ride about three miles or better down the road, so they could meet my other nieces and nephews and walk to school together. Then I would go and babysit for Mrs. Worsham. And in the afternoon, I would go back and pick them up on the bicycle.

When school was out in May, I said to Mrs. Worsham, "I'd like to have my diploma."

She said, "You have to bring me a sugar stamp." This was during World War II and sugar was being rationed.

So I said to her, "Okay." My mother gave me the stamp.

But my older sister Elsie had a lot of children, so I took the sugar stamp and I gave it to her so that she could have the sugar for her family. Her girls and I were very close; we were more like sisters than aunt and nieces. Because I did not give the stamp to Mrs. Worsham, she said she couldn't give my diploma to me. I did not get my diploma. My mother never did know what happened. I did not go into detail. But I felt this white woman had had enough of my free labor for one year. Compared to twenty-seven dollars a week, two dollars and fifty cents was just a little bit.

Still Young and Restless

I guess we were always restless. I know I was, after living in New Jersey and getting used to all its conveniences. We didn't have a lot of money, but we still enjoyed life. Now we knew what inside toilets and running water was. That was something we weren't used to before. So coming back to Virginia, we had to get used to the country life all over again.

From time to time I would go to New Jersey or Washington to visit my older sisters. They paid my way. I traveled by train two or three times a year. Then I would miss my mother so I would write home and have someone to write a letter to my sisters to say that Momma was sick. That way I could return when I got homesick without my sisters catching on.

Our Own Place

We worked hard like this for three years, and in the fall of 1943, we had enough money to buy a little place of our own. Tobacco prices were up; we were ready to purchase thirty-nine acres of land in Level Run.

The hard work had paid off. We had a place of our own.

Afterword

Like so many Southerners, I moved North again in 1952, with my husband Fred. This time I moved to Danbury, Connecticut where I could make a better living for my family. I started out doing domestic work; then I was a cook at a restaurant; then a worker in the hat factory. After that, I went to work for American Cyanamid where I stayed for seventeen years. There we achieved the good life that I had always prayed for. My children got a good education.

In 1971 I moved back to Richmond, Virginia to be closer to my home place and my relatives. I work as a private duty nurse. I've been blessed with my job, blessed with my six children, twelve grandchildren, and four great-grandchildren.

Blessed with good health, and a good life.

Acknowledgments

With thanks to God from whom all blessings flow; to my sister Lillie Margaret, who introduced us to a new life in Montclair, New Jersey, and provided the picture of my parents, Pency and George Walthall, for this book; to The Library of Virginia, The Valentine Museum, and Michael Rice for permission to use photographs; to our cousin Indiana Gregory for the picture of Clara Berger Gregory and Jerry Gregory; to the Portrait Place in Altavista, Virginia, especially Michelle Belzins, for her customer service; to daughters and granddaughters Patricia Lucille Forbes, Michelle Forbes, and Lisa Marie Rice for help transcribing and typing the manuscript; to our friend Jeanette Drake, who said, "Dorothy, this is wonderful, it must be published;" and to Diantha C. Thorpe, our editor, who agreed.

About the Photographs

Because Mabel's family were sharecroppers, there was little money for picture-taking. We have therefore combined snapshots from her family with photographs from The Library of Virginia and The Valentine Museum, Richmond, Virginia, as follows.

The photographs on the following pages are courtesy of The Library of Virginia: pages ii-iii, Tobacco-peg planting; page 47, Picking tobacco; page 53, Tobacco stripping; and page 56, Tobacco barn. Page 33, Children in Sunday dress, and page 44, Church outing, are courtesy of the Cook Collection/Valentine Museum. The rest of the photographs are courtesy of the authors: page 7, Pency and George Walthall; page 15, typical sharecropper house; page 19, Jerry and Clara Gregory, Mabel's grandparents; page 39, rural two-room schoolhouse; page 65, Mae West at age 7; page 71, sister Bea (right) and cousin Gladys;

page 83, sister Lillie Margaret in 1938;
page 91, Mabel at age 14; page 98, eight of
the eighteen children as adults, about 1960.
Left to right, top, Coolidge, Claude; second row,
Gracie, Katherine, Edna; third row, Virginia
Missouri, Mabel; bottom, Lillie Margaret.

--
B
Rice
R

Rice, Dorothy Marie,
  1948-

The seventeenth
  child.

DATE			